WITH THE UTMOST POSSIBLE DISPATCH

Poems of Nelson's Navy

WITH THE UTMOST POSSIBLE DISPATCH

Poems of Nelson's Navy

by

Harry Turner

*'In sea affairs, nothing is impossible,
and nothing improbable.'*

Horatio Nelson, 1804

SPELLMOUNT
Staplehurst

British Library Cataloguing in Publication Data:

A catalogue record for this book is available
from the British Library

Copyright © Harry Turner 2002

ISBN 1-86227-175-5

First published in the UK in 2002 by
Spellmount Limited
The Old Rectory
Staplehurst
Kent TN12 OAZ

Tel: 01580 893730
Fax: 01580 893731
E-mail: enquiries@spellmount.com
Website: www.spellmount.com

1 3 5 7 9 8 6 4 2

The right of Harry Turner to be identified
as the author of this work has been asserted by him
in accordance with the Copyright, Designs
and Patents Act 1988

Typeset in Palatino by MATS, Southend-on-Sea, Essex
Printed in Great Britain by
TJ International Ltd, Padstow, Cornwall

Contents

This book is dedicated
to British sailors of
all ranks past, present
and future.

Author's Note

I am grateful to the following sources which afforded me much inspiration when writing the poems.

Hibbert, Christopher, *Nelson, A Personal History*, London: Viking, 1994

Nicolas, Sir Harris, *Dispatches & Letters of Lord Nelson*, London: Colburn, 1846

Pocock, Tom, *Horatio Nelson*, London: Brockhampton, 1988

Pope, Dudley, *England Expects*, London: Weidenfeld & Nicolson, 1959

Southey, Robert, *The Life of Nelson*, London: Constable, 1999

White, Joshua, *Memoirs of Viscount Nelson*, London: Cundee, 1806

I am also indebted for the encouragement I received from Ian Fletcher, author and Peninsular War expert and for the unfailing courtesy and help I enjoyed at HMS *Victory* in Portsmouth, The National Maritime Museum at Greenwich and the British Museum in London.

Any errors or omissions are mine entirely although I have tried throughout to maintain historical, naval and geographical accuracy.

Introduction

There have been many books about great British heroes and, like most Englishmen, I have my favourites. Some acquired heroic stature by their deeds in later life, others seemed to have heroism bred in the bone. Nelson was one of the latter. He already had a fixed idea of his grand destiny when he was a callow youth.

Springing from a background of genteel poverty in rural Norfolk, Horatio Nelson set out to become the great legendary sailor we all read about at school.

Nelson, of course, left school at the age of 12, and his true education was at sea in a series of great wooden vessels that Britain had built in the eighteenth and nineteenth centuries.

I have chosen to re-tell the story of Nelson in verse because I felt it would be an appropriate form to carry the narrative forward and re-capture the romance and drama of life at sea during that extraordinary period of British history.

During my research for the book, I stood amazed at the ancient skills our forebears displayed in such things as ship-building, navigation and warfare. Just to look at HMS *Victory* sitting silently at Portsmouth docks is a truly moving experience.

The lives of ordinary sailors when aboard these mighty ships were hard and often cruel. Boys, scarcely more than children really, served in the King's navy and spent months at sea under conditions that today would be condemned as inhuman and degrading.

But Nelson, in addition to being a naval genius, was also a great man-manager, to use a modern term. He cared for his men deeply and his attention to detail when ordering provisions for his crews was proof of this. He knew that sailors properly fed and supported were crucial to success in battles at sea.

That Nelson was a flawed genius is beyond dispute, but then it is hard to contemplate any of our other great heroes like Wellington or Marlborough being paragons of virtue and rectitude – they were only too human.

Nelson's affair with Lady Hamilton caused great consternation at the time, even in an increasingly secular society, and many condemned her as a 'femme fatale'. Emma was, however, a remarkable woman, both feisty and independent.

The other striking thing about this period of history is how warfare was conducted in what can best be described as a gentlemanly fashion. Napoleon's admirals were mostly brave and talented and it is much to Nelson's credit that he defeated such a powerful and skilled enemy.

Just like another great hero the Duke of Wellington, Nelson experienced frustration throughout his career with his bureaucratic masters in Parliament and at the Admiralty.

He was also, like Wellington, a prolific writer of dispatches, letters and reports. After losing his right arm, he forced himself to write left-handed with a degree of perseverence that is quite breathtaking.

Although fiercely loyal to his King and country, Nelson was something of a maverick when it came to interpreting orders from his superiors. His tactics, when engaging the enemy at sea, often broke the mould of conventional warfare, particularly at the Battle of Trafalgar. Driven by his sense of destiny, his 'radiant orb', he occasionally felt that his genius was not fully recognised by his peers. This frustration manifested itself in bouts of irritation which fell just short of rebellion. In the end however, his sense of duty and his sheer courage saw him through.

The poems in this book, which run chronologically, can only give what I hope is a flavour of Nelson's life and times and capture something of the atmosphere prevailing then, when Britannia truly Ruled the Waves.

Harry Turner
Deepcut, Surrey, 2002

The Poems

1

HMS *VICTORY*

Majestic she rose in the swell,
Spume skidding along her sleek sides,
Her gilded stern with its trident and shields,
Defiant of Neptune's worst tides.
Awake my soul and with the sun
Thy daily stage of duty run.

With canvas billowing high overhead,
And her topsails and gallants so proud,
Her very appearance proclaiming
'Britannia' in a voice clear and loud.
Awake my soul and with the sun
Thy daily stage of duty run.

She loomed high and mighty,
Her cannons still hot,
Crammed with bare-chested sailors,
Gunpowder and shot.
Awake my soul and with the sun
Thy daily stage of duty run.

And the stench from her decks
Could be smelled from afar,
'Twas tobacco and sweat,
Human waste, salt and tar.
Awake my soul and with the sun
Thy daily stage of duty run.

While far down below,
Rough sailors would sing,
Their voices well coarsened
By ship's rum and gin.
Awake my soul and with the sun
Thy daily stage of duty run.

Oh Lord, save this vessel
And all those who are in it,
And let's whip old Frenchie
In less than a minute.
Awake my soul and with the sun
Thy daily stage of duty run.

For when we're at sea
We will all serve our King,
But when on dry land
Different songs we may sing.
Awake my soul and with the sun
Thy daily stage of duty run.

Thus when shore at last
Draws clear into sight,
We'll carouse and we'll booze
For the rest of the night.
Awake my soul and with the sun
Thy daily stage of duty run.

We'll find us fat wenches
By the dozen or more,
All as plump and as ripe
As a young Portsmouth whore.
Awake my soul and with the sun
Thy daily stage of duty run.

We'll lay us all down
With these sweet saucy misses,
And from their wet lips
We'll pluck many hot kisses.
Awake my soul and with the sun
Thy daily stage of duty run.

They'll taste the dry salt
On our cheeks and our whiskers,
And we shall demand –
'Now bring out your sisters'!
Awake my soul and with the sun
Thy daily stage of duty run.

Thus hungry matelots will feed,
And satisfy each stifled need,
And roistering and finest ale
Will be companion to this tale.
Awake my soul and with the sun
Thy daily stage of duty run.

When sailors have been long at sea,
They must slake their raging thirsts,
Not casually like gentlemen,
But in short frenzied bursts.
Awake my soul and with the sun
Thy daily stage of duty run.

For soon again the cannon's roar,
The creak of timber, splashing oar,
Thus pleasures brief are put aside,
And Englishmen sail with the tide.
Awake my soul and with the sun
Thy daily stage of duty run.

2

FIRST TIME ABOARD

The first time on a British ship,
Creates a unique feeling,
The sights and smells and clanging bells,
Send all the senses reeling.

The shouts of men with muscled backs,
As coils of rope are lifted,
And oaken casks with waists of steel,
By calloused hands are shifted.

The smell of sweat and boiling meat,
Of tar, wet rope and tallow,
The creak of timbers, flapping sails,
The gun ports tight and narrow.

And sailors heave aboard supplies,
To stack below the decks,
Black pepper, mustard and salt pork,
Meticulously checked.

There's sugar, vinegar and flour,
And even calf's foot jellies
For sailors bound for mountainous seas,
Need food to fill their bellies.

Great puncheons of bread are stacked,
Each one of awesome size,
And wine that they called 'Blackstrap',
That brings tears to sailors' eyes.

Thick blocks of farmyard butter,
In muslin all wrapped tight,
And countless sacks of onions,
'Gainst scurvy these will fight.

And mighty slabs of holystone,
And Portland stone in blocks,
To scour the decks when they're at sea,
And far from English docks.

There's so much work still to be done
Before they all set sail,
As bum-boats crammed with women,
Bring out bladders filled with ale.

Some still may stay aboard the ship,
If the captain should agree,
But women on a battleship,
Aren't good when out at sea.

Oakum had been hammered in
To bolster up the hull,
And from this hard and sweating toil,
There's scarcely been a lull.

Coated thick with linseed oil,
With whitelead too – and tar,
The ship's almighty timbers,
Must be spick, and up to par.

The masts aloft and rigging,
Each gun-port and each block,
Must be tested most severely,
While they still bob in the dock.

Her hull is sheathed in copper,
Like a giant cooking pot,
For after weary weeks at sea,
Unprotected wood will rot.

The old salts are familiar
With what trials may lie ahead,
How the weevils and the maggots
Will devastate their bread.

How butter will turn rancid
When the temperature is hot,
And is smeared upon the rigging
To alleviate dry rot.

How tubs are filled with urine
That the sailors have just passed,
To be stored up by the bowsprit,
Just a few feet from the mast.

How their vests and socks and underclothes
Will need many vigorous rubs,
How ammonia will bleach them clean,
As they swirl in these foul tubs.

The sailor will write letters home,
Saying, 'Mother what of this,
I'm washing all my shirts and stuff,
In a bath of sailor's piss'.

He will need to observe quite closely,
Every futtock, chain and joint,
Each tangle of the rigging,
Every bolt and screw and point.

He must recognise just everything
That's below decks and above,
Know the names of every ship's part,
Treat them like his lady love.

The poop deck and belfry,
The bowsprit and stern,
The bilge pumps and capstan,
There's still so much to learn.

There's the mizzenmast and mainmast
And the magazine and more,
And the sailors' squalid sleeping place,
Where exhausted men will snore.

There's the howsers and the anchor
A massive solid weight,
And the square trays made from timber,
That will serve as dinner plate.

He will see the stinking manger
With its cows and pigs and sheep,
And when he feels quite homesick
'Tis here alone he'll weep.

The guns up on the gun decks,
Stand slick-black, shiny bright,
Made of solid English iron,
Mouths gaping wide to fight.

He'll ponder all these awesome things
As he roams around the ship,
They'll become much more familiar
As he makes each separate trip.

He'll learn to be aware now
Of all the different trades,
That constitute a ship's crew,
Of their ranks and various grades.

The carpenters and armourers,
Sail-makers and the cooks,
The officers who navigate
As they study charts and books.

And if he's sailing with the fleets,
He'll need to recognise,
The various ships who sail with him,
Their gun-strength, speed and size.

Are they frigates, are they galliots,
Are they luggers, are they sloops,
Are they brigantines or billanders,
Are they sailing now in groups?

And thus the raw young Englishman
With his dreams and starry hopes,
Will soon be institutionalised
As he starts to learn the ropes.

So when he stands upon the deck,
Emotions strangely mixed,
He senses with each swelling wave,
His destiny is fixed.

Sea-salt is in his bloodstream now,
And all his landlocked notions
Evaporate like cannon smoke,
With his new life on the oceans.

3

YOUNG HORACE

His figure small and slender,
His voice a Norfolk brogue,
You'd not have marked this fellow out
As a hero or a rogue.

Yet deep behind that modest chest,
Beat a heart of English oak,
And a steely sense of destiny,
He wore just like a cloak.

Just where would a hero choose to live?
Which rolling pastoral county,
What tree-lined park would satisfy
And provide domestic bounty?

Not Leicestershire or Lincolnshire,
Or Staffordshire or Devon,
Which corner of green England then,
Would be his piece of heaven?

His choice may shock or just amuse,
But one thing can be certain,
Not many people realise,
That Nelson's choice was Merton.

A hero and adulterer,
A cocksure pompous bantam,
His figure, unlike Hercules,
Was slimmer than a phantom.

Thus from a very early age,
When examining his story,
Young Nelson was quite openly
Obsessed with dreams of glory.

11

He wrote and spoke without constraint,
He never was a stoic,
Of daring deeds on foaming seas,
His role of course – heroic.

A letter penned in Nelson's hand,
All modesty forsaken,
Once claimed to the Duke of Clarence
That 'He'd never been mistaken'.

His trust in providence divine,
Made Nelson even bolder,
He felt the mighty hand of God,
Upon his slender shoulder.

When he was young and innocent,
Some thought an ugly duckling,
He made a plea to go to sea
To his uncle, Maurice Suckling.

Now Captain Suckling pondered this,
He clearly was uneasy,
How 'poor weak Horace' would survive,
Made him a trifle queasy.

And yet before the age of twelve,
His first ship he had boarded,
Exposed to the life of a matelot,
That was both tough and sordid.

This first ship was at Chatham,
Where to the crew's surprise,
His schoolboy boasts of future fame
Drew groans of mocking cries.

In the sixty-four gun *Raisonnable*,
Was where he learnt the ropes,
Which fired the young man's fantasies
And bolstered up his hopes.

'Twas thus this tough apprenticeship
That taught him to survive,
Helped form his future character,
Personality and drive.

No person in those far off days,
Of seventeen-seventy-one,
Would have dared to forecast that this lad,
England's hero would become.

But now his place in history,
Is gloriously secure,
Like Marlborough and Wellington,
His name will long endure.

4

ARCTIC INCIDENT

'Twas the British Navy's proudest claim,
Their patriotic boast,
That they could sail the seven seas
To the farthest foreign coast.

The invention by an Englishman,
John Harrison by name,
Of the means to measure longitude,
Brought him plaudits, wealth and fame.

His fine marine chronometer,
Had passed each rigorous test,
Enabling sailors out at sea,
To check both east and west.

Thus accuracy was now the key,
To every ship of line,
Making easy for the men afloat,
Their position to define.

It was in the good ship *Carcass*,
In seventeen-seventy-three,
That Nelson, still a callow youth,
Sailed to the Arctic Sea.

One evening on an ice floe,
And accompanied by a mate,
Young Nelson sought adventure,
And very nearly sealed his fate.

He had spotted on the floating ice,
A plump white polar bear,
And resolved at once to shoot it,
As it stood silhouetted there.

But Nelson's musket failed to fire
And the massive, furry beast,
Turned snarling to the foolish lad,
On his English flesh to feast.

But fate, thank God, had intervened,
As through the Arctic night,
A single cannon shot was heard,
That set the bear to flight.

The Captain of the *Carcass*,
A doughty, grizzled salt,
Had noticed Nelson's daring prank,
And resolved to call a halt.

One cannon shot was just required
To save young Nelson's neck,
And later, trembling fearfully,
He'd face his Captain on the deck.

'Just what the hell in blazes
Do you think that you were doing?'
Cried Captain Lutwidge angrily,
'I saw the beast pursuing.'

'One swipe from him, you reckless lad,
One hug, that's all, one bite,
And you'd have been a tasty meal,
His supper for tonight.'

Young Nelson now could clearly see
His Captain in a lather,
'I only hoped to skin the beast
And take it home to Father.'

At this old Captain Lutwidge smiled,
And put a hand on Nelson's shoulder,
'You'll do worse things I do declare
Before you grow much older.'

'Now get below and smarten up,
A tot of rum you've earned,
If from this mad experience
A tot of sense you've learned.'

And thus it ended happily,
This cheery sailor's tale,
That soon became a legend,
When old salts supped their ale.

PALMAM QUI MERUIT FERAT

Nelson

Lord Nelson

5

THE RADIANT ORB, 1775

Beneath old India's azure sky,
And equatorial heat,
Where tigers in abundance roamed,
And man was merely meat.

'Twas here that Englishmen were plagued,
By ague, flux and fly,
Where maladies malodorous
Caused countless men to die.

By Bombay's fever ridden coast,
Beneath a roasting sun,
Young Nelson too was stricken down,
And felt he would succumb.

His colleagues all feared for the worst,
The surgeon gave a sigh,
And sent him on the voyage home,
Convinced that he would die.

In his hammock he lay feverish,
His body racked with pain,
It took him many days and nights,
His consciousness to gain.

A brief respite at Simonstown,
Close to the famous Cape,
Led Nelson to believe at last,
From death he would escape.

Though still depressed and weakly,
On the Atlantic journey north,
His mind was in a turmoil,
Confused thoughts were bursting forth.

Would he rise in his profession?
Had his efforts been in vain?
Would his epitaph be modest?
Would the world forget his name?

Thus 'twas in the good ship *Dolphin*,
That young Nelson had a vision,
As if some spirit from above,
In his breast had now arisen.

His destiny was clear and bold,
Like a radiant orb or sun,
For King and country he would strive
And a hero he'd become.

He'd face down every danger,
And subjugate each foe,
This vision now enveloped him
In a patriotic glow.

By the time he reached olde England,
He was healthy, fit and keen,
An extraordinary metamorphosis
From how he'd lately been.

He'd place his trust in providence,
And God would be his guide,
His King would be his patron
And he'd serve them both with pride.

Let the devil do his damnedest now,
With his awesome storms at sea,
For Nelson knew with certainty,
England's hero he would be.

6

THE POWDER MONKEYS

They were all very small, though they later grew tall
In the service of their Sovereign King,
They would scamper and run, from the rise of the sun
As to gunners fresh powder they'd bring.

At the cannons' first roar they stood steady,
In the smoke and the noise and the heat,
Dressed in rags like a chimney sweep's helper,
With no shoes on to cover their feet.

Down ladders of rope they descended,
To the ship's magazine far below,
Where they'd gather up small bags of powder,
And serve every gun in its row.

These urchins who toiled in the navy,
Who performed menial tasks by the score,
Who emptied the slops of the sailors,
Were just ten years old, seldom more.

Some fell in the fiercesome sea battles,
Some grew sick in the tropics and died,
But those who survived grew to manhood,
Became gunners themselves, full of pride.

It is hard now to comprehend clearly,
How Britain's control of the sea,
Was dependent, in part, on the stoutness of heart
Of young children who heroes would be.

And with passage of the years,
And surging tides and oceans,
We still salute and pay tribute,
With deeply felt emotions.

To those skinny powder monkeys,
Whose nimbleness and pluck,
On Neptune's vastly foaming deep,
Enhanced olde England's luck.

7

POST NUBILA PHOEBUS*

As Nelson reached the English coast
In seventeen-eighty-seven,
He vowed a hero he'd become,
A promise made in heaven.

A new command was what he sought,
To serve the English King,
On oceans deep his pledge he'd keep,
He craved no other thing.

But the Admiralty in London,
Were impervious to his wishes,
Young men who sought command, it seemed,
Were as plentiful as fishes.

At Burnham Thorpe in Norfolk,
He turned his hand to farming,
He'd come to this bucolic bliss
In pastoral peace most charming.

But after many months ashore,
Frustrated there he rested,
Of country life he'd had his fill,
His patience sorely tested.

When Nelson was becalmed at sea,
And no wind filled his sails,
He'd wait in peace on silent decks,
And pray for fruitful gales.

*After clouds comes sunshine.

But taken from his ocean home
And far from wind and tide,
He feels as if his heart is stalled
Along with hope and pride.

The weary years of idleness,
Spin cobwebs in his soul,
At close of day, a prayer he'll say,
'God help me reach my goal'.

But then one day a messenger
Arrives on horse-drawn coach,
His spirits soar, while at the door
He sees the man approach.

A document is offered,
Closed with a seal of wax,
With eager hands he seizes it,
Of patience now, he lacks.

'Tis a summons from the Admiralty,
Most gloriously clear,
Lord Chatham has commanded him
In London to appear.

A ship at last, oh glorious day!
Let church bells peal unfettered,
May rafters ring, and angels sing,
This news cannot be bettered.

His ship, the *Agamemnon*,
With guns of sixty-four,
Will face the revolutionary French,
He can scarcely ask for more.

He'll serve a British Admiral,
A hero great and good,
An inspiration to all officers,
The redoubtable Lord Hood.

To Naples then, he sails at speed,
With high hopes now of glory,
But destiny awaits him there
To complicate his story.

He meets the British Envoy's wife,
And is at once quite smitten.
For fruit is tastier, it's said
When eating it's forbidden.

Dear Lady Hamilton herself,
Vivacious, bright and charming,
Is flattered by Horatio's glance,
She finds it quite disarming.

But more of this alas, anon,
While Cupid's arrow pauses,
For Nelson has much work afoot,
With patriotic causes.

He sails off with a squadron,
To face his old French foe,
First Toulon then to Tunis
Is where his ships must go.

Thus battle follows battle,
As he tackles each new task,
Every order sent by good Lord Hood,
Is executed fast.

There's Bastia and Calvi,
Where Nelson is distinguished.
Each time he runs against the French,
Their efforts are extinguished.

But then his luck is thwarted,
As cruel fate plays its hand,
He is wounded, not aboard his ship,
But standing on dry land.

His mission is straightforward,
He must dominate the town,
And by using massive siege guns,
He can blow these walls right down.

But the guns must now be grounded,
And manhandled to the shore,
Thus for dozens of the matelots,
It's a heavy, sweating chore.

Over boulder-strewn inlets,
And up steep rocky slopes,
Men are hauling great cannons
With winches and ropes.

But progress is painful,
So much work to be done,
As they build up each battery
In the heat of the sun.

At last the work is finished,
As each battery is now ready,
And behind the ramparts built of soil,
The gunners all stand steady.

The bombardment is ferocious,
And smoke billows in the sky,
As from those city walls, one hears
The French guns' sharp reply.

Some cannon balls just whistle past,
And continue overhead,
But others strike their targets,
Killing scores of men stone dead.

And the firing goes on wildly,
Until the French are forced to yield,
And Calvi now surrenders,
Thus its fate is safely sealed.

But during this fierce battle,
As flames light up the sky,
Nelson stands close besides his gunners
And gives a rallying cry.

And thus before the Frenchmen
Acknowledge their defeat,
A bouncing shot of cannon,
Explodes by Nelson's feet.

The impact is ferocious,
Sending sharp stones flying high,
And a jagged piece strikes Nelson,
And pierces his right eye.

Blood streaked, in pain and blinded,
He shrugs off this hideous blow,
Optimistic and defiant
He will not retire below.

But later on he senses,
With frustration and with dread,
That he is virtually blinded,
In the right eye of his head.

And now with typical courage,
He simply spurns despair,
'The left one's working splendidly',
He'll heroically declare.

So this mighty fight for Calvi
Is over now and finished.
Nelson's triumph is quite clear to all,
And his fame is undiminished.

But later on in Whitehall,
In the famed *London Gazette*,
Admiral Hood's report of the battle
Causes Nelson much regret.

He feels that his role in the battle,
And his skill in reducing the town,
Has been seriously under-acknowledged.
He feels snubbed and badly let down.

Bewildered, surprised and embarrassed,
Resentment envelopes his soul.
Why couldn't Lord Hood, a man true and good,
Simply recognise Nelson's great role?

But the mood he feels is just transient,
Though emotionally painful and brief,
And he makes a vow, that he cannot allow
To be swamped by self pity and grief.

So he looks ahead now to his future,
Finds his life's dream is still quite intact.
It's on oceans he'll triumph and conquer,
No regrets then, and no looking back.

8

DEAREST EMMA

She was only a blacksmith's daughter,
But a woman determined and strong,
Though from humble beginnings in Cheshire,
'Twas ambition that drove her along.

Not for her, simple life in a cottage,
While shire horses whinnied and neighed.
At the age of fourteen, with the poise of a queen,
Future plans for her life had been made.

Thus to London she travelled quite boldly,
Was employed as a young children's maid,
Who was not there for long, and soon she was gone
Seeking work much less boring and staid.

She located employment in Mayfair,
In fashionable Arlington Street,
Where the sons of the rich sought their pleasures,
In houses both smart and discreet.

The lady in charge was called Kelly,
A madam of legendary fame,
Who found her young protégée Emma,
Took swiftly to life on the game.

By the use of her charms and in eager swain's arms,
She was coquettish and popular too,
But her stay here was brief, and to Ma Kelly's grief,
Was engaged soon in something quite new.

At the temple of 'Health and of Hymen',
A mansion devoted to love,
She attended the noble and high born,
Cupid's angel come down from above.

This palace exotic and charming,
Had a grand and 'celestial bed',
Where couples infertile and barren,
Could conceive a child – it is said.

By the age of sixteen and full bodied,
Dear Emma had now raised her game.
She had moved to a cottage in Sussex,
'Twas her next step to glittering fame.

Her lover was a man called Sir Harry,
A kindly old codger it's true,
Who when he'd exhausted his pleasure,
Was perplexed at what next he might do.

But by now dear Emma was pregnant,
And soon her first baby was born,
So Sir Harry, like many before him,
'Twixt lust and self interest was torn.

He had no desire to continue
With Emma or now with her child,
So the cynical plan, by this selfish old man,
Was cunning, immoral and wild.

He located a friend who was lonely,
One who's love life was empty and bleak,
The man was Charles Greville, and though not a devil,
Like Sir Harry, was morally weak.

He installed her in London at Edgware,
Where he told all his friends she made tea,
But this lie was transparent as water,
As his mistress she soon was to be.

All went well till Charles Greville discovered,
An heiress he wanted to wed,
So he had to dispose of poor Emma,
She'd no longer be warming his bed.

He turned to his favourite uncle,
A man of distinction and style,
Our envoy in far away Naples,
Who though clever, was quite without guile.

Thus Sir William at last was persuaded,
To make Emma a most welcome guest,
So she was installed with her mother,
At Charles Greville's impassioned request.

Life at the Court there in Naples
With its banquets and soirées galore,
Gave Emma the life of a lady,
As she shrugged off her past as a whore.

Although at first quite cautious,
And quite reticent up to a fault,
Sir William still treated dear Emma,
As a favoured young guest when at Court.

But he very soon had surrendered
To Emma's most sensuous charms,
And overnight gossips in Naples,
Knew he'd eventually melt in her arms.

And thus by and by it did happen,
Dear Emma took vows as his wife,
Becoming a most brilliant hostess
And the light of old Hamilton's life.

She mixed with the high born and wealthy,
Including the King and the Queen,
The latter she'd flatter, and this didn't matter,
No one gave a fig what she'd been.

Now the high point of Naples society,
Was a caricature of excess,
With Emma a glittering focus,
Adding spice to imperiousness.

After meals both gargantuan and vulgar,
Where wines were consumed by the gross,
The Queen showed affection for Emma,
And the two became friends, even close.

Sir William observed this serenely,
Loved his young wife's new glitter and pluck,
While others might titter, some even felt bitter,
Saying 'Emma's as common as muck'.

For Emma still spoke like a fishwife,
In an accent both loud and uncouth,
And the women in Court held their fans up,
To whisper the sins of her youth.

But Emma was blithely impervious,
Ignoring the sniggers and taunts
As she cut a swathe in society
Through Naples' most glamorous haunts.

Her confidence now as a hostess,
Won Sir William's approval and praise,
When she struck an 'attitude' his genuine gratitude
Was writ large in the warmth of his gaze.

This extravagant high-style performance,
Like a solitary ballet or mime,
Though maladroit, gauche and pretentious,
Was a fashionable 'thing' of the time.

When Nelson first made her acquaintance,
He found her both bright and quite charming,
Her wit was as sharp as a needle, and yet
Her sex-appeal doubly disarming.

A passage of years came between them,
Before they would meet once again.
And Nelson's repute as a hero,
Had now reached a much higher plain.

He was one of olde England's clear favourites,
A warrior famous and strong,
A superman, even an icon,
Who it seemed would never do wrong.

But through years of the greatest indulgence
Of feasting and fine vintage wine,
Dear Emma was heavy and corpulent
Though her face still a picture divine.

It was chemistry, potent and fatal
That captured Horatio's heart,
As Cupid released his taut bowstring
And fired off his amorous dart.

Their love affair was called scandalous,
Adulterous, wicked and shaming,
And Sir William, a gentleman cuckold,
Stood back meekly, never complaining.

But other observers in England,
Said that Horatio should warrant rebuke,
Condemning his conduct severely
And demanding to bring him to book.

But when he returned home to England,
With Sir William as well as his wife,
The fact that this trio, with confident brio,
Lived together was no cause of strife.

Nelson's legendary skill as an Admiral,
His courage, his dash and success,
Some compared to his role as a lover,
Dubbed him guilty of carnal excess.

It was a strangely domestic arrangement,
This mutual ménage à trois,
Attracting moral rebukes, from both peasants and dukes
Who felt Nelson had now gone too far.

That Sir William was clearly a cuckold,
Was impossible now to ignore,
But he still remained, though ageing and strained,
Blind to truth that his wife was a whore.

Thus at length when Sir William was ailing,
And approaching the end of his life,
He still believed Nelson a hero,
And no more than a friend to his wife.

Dear Emma of course was a widow,
And found to her shame and her cost,
That her previous place in society,
Once so great, was regrettably lost.

In spite of the sneers and the mocking
That Nelson would learn to endure,
To honour her name, he made it quite plain,
Their affair was ostensibly pure.

But perchance just a few could accept this strange view,
To others their affair was just odd,
As Nelson exclaimed – 'we cannot be blamed,
We've not sinned in the eyes of our God.'

Both Emma and he took the sacrament,
Standing solemn and still, side-by-side,
Though no hymns did they sing, when each gave a ring,
'Twas a token of love and of pride.

Then followed the stern call of duty,
Requiring the lovers to part.
Poor Emma was grieving at Horatio's leaving,
A dagger had been plunged in her heart.

But Nelson resolved he must still serve his King,
Knowing duty for him was supreme.
Their parting was tearful and Emma was fearful,
And she let out a pitiful scream.

'I know you'll be killed, I can sense it,
My forebodings are awful and stark,
If you leave me now, I'm swearing a vow,
My life will be shrouded and dark.'

But Nelson by now had departed,
On the road at the first crack of dawn,
In a rattling coach, as his port he'd approach,
'Twixt duty and love he was torn.

To God up in heaven he uttered a prayer:
'On my humble head mercy I seek,
But if I die soon, just grant me this boon,
Protect Emma each day of the week.

'For she'll be alone when I've parted,
Send an angel to stand by her side,
For I can face death, with my ultimate breath,
Knowing Emma's my spiritual bride.'

And thus when he died she did mourn him,
Wearing cockades of black and a veil,
And a lock of his hair to remember,
Plus a fragment of *Victory*'s sail.

And later when dear Emma died,
One thing is known for certain,
She may have died in Calais, but
Her spirit lives in Merton.

A daughter, Horatia, was born to Emma and Nelson on 29 January 1801 at 23 Piccadilly, London. Nelson saw his child only occasionally. After Emma died in Calais in 1815, Horatia returned to England. In 1822 she married a curate, Philip Ward, and their first son was christened Horatio Nelson. Horatia never acknowledged that Lady Emma Hamilton was her mother. Horatia died on 6 March 1881.

9

EL CASTILLO DE LA IMMACULADA CONCEPCIÓN, 1779

With the bloom of youth still on his cheek
And his reputation growing,
The navy's faith in their precocious son,
Was little short of glowing.

As Post-Captain in the *Hinchinbrooke*,
In this new role he was cast,
The ship, with eight and twenty guns,
Was a frigate sleek and fast.

By the jungles of Nicaragua,
Inhospitable and dank,
Runs the mighty river of San Juan
With tall forests on each bank.

Up river lay a Spanish port
They'd been ordered to attack.
And Nelson knew, as they set sail,
There'd be no turning back.

The Spaniards had deployed their troops
On both sides of the river,
From the island stronghold in between,
Resistance they'd deliver.

Although the British plan was clear,
To separate the Spanish,
They'd need to move with lightning speed,
Or their one main chance might vanish.

Commander of the British troops
Who would lead the expedition,
Was the gallant Colonel Polson,
A man blessed with erudition.

When first he met with Nelson,
Cool tactics he'd employ,
For Nelson, barely twenty-one
Was just a 'light-haired boy'.

This youth of palest countenance,
His figure neat, but slight,
Was to command the seven transport ships,
And lead them to the fight.

In a week of high humidity,
And blistering tropic heat,
The assault upon the Spanish fort
Seemed doomed to face defeat.

With some boats overloaded,
In the turgid jungle water,
Young Nelson knew, without his help,
The troops might soon face slaughter.

With fifty sailors and marines,
He joined the ground assault,
And after fighting fiercely,
Seized an outpost of the fort.

As they set batteries on the shore,
For the final, vital fight,
The clouds grew ominous overhead,
Turning daytime into night.

The heavens opened with a roar,
Torrential rain exploding.
But still those soldiers on the shore,
Their guns continued loading.

But came their hour of triumph then,
As the fortress fell at last.
Tho' Nelson felt a surge of pain,
It was not to be his last.

And then convulsions seized him,
Pain lanced throughout his head,
For dysentery had struck him down,
With no help, he'd soon be dead.

But willing hands took over,
Placing Nelson in a boat,
And he lay shivering, feverishly
Under a sailor's coat.

Thus victory had been secured,
The Spanish fortress taken,
Though Nelson's part was finished now,
As he lay, pale and shaken.

And back aboard the *Hinchinbrooke*,
Command he now relinquished,
To Collingwood, a trusted friend,
A sailor most distinguished.

Another chapter in his life,
Another triumph noted,
Establishing beyond all doubt,
To glory he was devoted.

He'd convalesce in England,
After a brief spell in Jamaica,
Recovering fully, as he spurned
This chance to meet his maker.

El Castillo de la Immaculada Concepción was the Spanish fort on the San Juan river that separated the Spanish troops between Nicaragua and Costa Rica. Thus, if Spanish territories in Mexico and the south could be split, the British hoped to enlarge their holding into a potential colony.

10

SANTA CRUZ, 1797

On the eve of the great battle,
Nelson dined aboard in style,
Knowing fierce and bloody conflict
Would engulf him in a while.

Unperturbed and quite avuncular,
He joked and sipped his wine,
Assuring senior officers
That their prospects were 'damned fine'.

A league or so away there lay
The coast of Santa Cruz,
With its mighty towering Citadel,
'Twas a prize they couldn't lose.

Though confident of victory,
Nelson knew that he must ask
For great courage and great sacrifice
From his men who faced this task.

At eleven in the evening,
With the night as black as pitch,
Nelson hoped and prayed the plans he'd laid
Would succeed without a hitch.

With his captains and their squadrons
As they prepared to sail,
He was focused and exultant
With God's help, how could they fail?

The plan was plain and simple,
They would land upon the mole,
Then proceed on foot like soldiers,
The great Citadel, their goal.

But the Spanish were expecting them
Behind those granite walls,
With a mass of heavy weaponry,
Grapeshot and cannon balls.

Alarm bells clanged in lofty towers,
And braziers were lit,
As several British in their boats
Received a direct hit.

As cannon roared and muskets cracked,
The boats approached the shore.
Some floundered in the raging surf
And sank to the ocean's floor.

But those who made it to the mole,
And scrambled on dry land,
Faced massive opposition there
As they battled hand-to-hand.

But British tars give of their best
When opposition's stout,
They fought like demons hot from hell,
And it soon became a rout.

The Spanish guns upon the mole
Were spiked and cast aside,
But the cannons in the Citadel
Poured forth their deadly tide.

British sailors fell like ninepins
In that lethal hail of lead,
Brave young matelots and midshipmen
Cut down and left for dead.

Some boats had splintered on the rocks
And men hurled in the water,
As musket fire from Spanish troops
Continued with the slaughter.

As Nelson's cutter reached the mole,
He planned to disembark,
But fate deployed its awful hand
As he scrambled in the dark.

A shot smashed through his elbow,
Splintering the bone,
He fell back in the swaying boat
Without a single groan.

But as he fell he caught his sword,
His left hand gripped it tight,
He wouldn't drop this weapon
For the remainder of the night.

The sword had been a gift to him
From a man he much admired,
His uncle, Maurice Suckling,
When the gallant man retired.

But his stepson, young Josiah
Was promptly by his side,
And deftly placed a tourniquet
To stem the crimson tide.

At length he was persuaded
To sail back to his ship,
And once aboard the *Theseus*,
The surgeons took a grip.

They saw the shattered elbow
With its lacerated flesh,
Which they briskly amputated
While his adrenalin was fresh.

Meantime, the landing parties,
Less than seven hundred strong,
Were repulsed by Spanish gunfire
In a battle fierce and long.

The garrison at Santa Cruz,
Which had eight thousand men,
Could not be bluffed or beaten,
Though the British tried again.

At last the British casualties,
On that bleak and awful night,
Rose to hundreds killed or wounded
In a brutal, bruising fight.

So the fortress stood inviolate,
While smoke plumed overhead,
And the British limped back to their ships
After burying their dead.

And later in the *Theseus*,
The wounded Nelson wrote,
'I'm a burden to my countrymen',
In a plaintive, tragic note.

But the courage of the fellow
Was now plain for all to see,
As he scribbled with his left hand,
While his ship bobbed on the sea.

His commander, Lord St Vincent,
To whom the note was sent,
Refused to say that Nelson's day,
Was over, lost or spent.

So after convalescence
And months of nagging pain,
The one-armed hero did return
To serve his King again.

11

THE VICTOR OF THE NILE, 1798

The British were cleared for action,
With port-lids open wide,
The guns run out, the hammocks rolled
'Gainst bulwarks down each side.

Packed tight in nets defensively,
Flying splinters to resist,
And sails were wetted against fire,
No item had been missed.

All hatches down, save only two
Where powder monkeys worked,
To bring up bags to feed the guns,
No beardless lad had shirked.

Damp sand was strewn upon the decks
Where sailor's blood might drip,
And naked feet, in battle's heat
Might stumble, trip or slip.

The captains on their quarterdecks,
Each gunner by his gun,
The surgeons in the cockpit
Out of the broiling sun,

The carpenters and repair men,
Poised on the orlop decks,
And lieutenants with their swords drawn,
Knotted kerchiefs round their necks.

The gun crews stripped and sweating,
Big men with muscled backs,
By convex line of cannon,
Standing eager to attack.

For they had finally found the French,
After gruelling weeks at sea,
And their elusive enemy
At last was plain to see.

From Malta and Koroni,
Hard by the coast of Greece,
The British had pursued them,
Their zeal would never cease.

Though Nelson's colleague Troubridge
Had seized a large French brig,
It carried only casks of wine,
As a prize 'twas far from big.

For Nelson wanted to engage
Napoleon's fighting fleet.
French ships of line, would just be fine
For the British to defeat.

Thus eastward had the navy sailed,
To the Delta or the Nile,
To Aboukir on the Egyptian coast,
Moving smoothly and with style.

On the very first day of August,
In the afternoon at two,
Midshipman Elliot, through his glass,
Scanned the skyline clear and blue.

He surely doubted what he saw,
His heart then missed a beat,
For anchored at this ancient port,
Bobbed the ships of the whole French fleet.

He shouted to the quarterdeck,
Cried 'Enemy in sight'!
The signal flags were hoisted
In anticipation of the fight.

The news was passed from ship to ship,
At last they'd face the test,
And utmost joy, quite unalloyed,
Seemed to animate every breast.

As Nelson now, elated,
Paced restlessly on deck,
He issued orders to his men,
Each detail he would check.

'Before this time tomorrow',
He's reported to have said,
'I'll either be a peer my lads,
Or alternatively – dead!'

Although much plagued with toothache,
He was unable to sit still,
The approaching clash of arms he felt,
Was the ultimate warrior's thrill.

Two seamen quartered at a gun,
Not far from Nelson's side,
Had openly discussed their fate
With stoic British pride.

'Damn me,' said one, a burly tar,
'If we don't beat them Jack,
It's sure as hell that they'll beat us,
There 'aint no going back.'

Hearing this from simple men
Whose lives might soon be lost,
Made Nelson swear a fervent oath,
He'd win at any cost.

A north-west wind had filled their sails,
But Nelson knew for sure,
They still faced hours of sailing hard
Before they reached the shore.

They couldn't yet engage the French,
Though clearly in their sight,
For they had to be in gunshot range
Before starting any fight.

While meantime Admiral Brueys,
Who commanded the French fleet,
Had anchored all his vessels there,
'Twas a tactic he deemed neat.

He'd formed a floating fortress,
Between the shoals and shore,
An obstacle impregnable,
Of this he was quite sure.

On seeing such formations,
Nelson felt a spurt of joy.
The battle tactics he had planned,
Were now ready to deploy.

At three o'clock that afternoon,
Beneath an azure sky,
Nelson's orders were quite simple,
'We prevail or else we die.'

We must attack their end of line,
Then strike at van and centre,
Let every man give of his best,
As through fires of hell we enter.

So now the lines of British ships,
Prepared for the assault,
A formidable flotilla
That turned in towards the port.

These mighty ships sailed past the shoals,
Though Nelson had no maps.
Sheer seamanship of the highest cut,
Prevented most mishaps.

Save Troubridge in *Culloden*,
Who in spite of skill and pluck,
Was grounded on a sandbank,
A stroke of damned bad luck.

But Nelson in the *Vanguard*,
Was resolved to still attack,
Flanked by *Zealous* and *Goliath*,
And with more ships at his back,

Then came the crack and flash of guns,
As cannons belched out flame,
Dismasting one of Brueys' ships,
Rendering several others lame.

La Sérieuse was duly sunk,
An awesome, broken wreck,
As sailors slithered desperately
On her tilting, splintered deck.

The enemy flagship *L'Orient*,
A massive, looming sight,
Was broadside now with blazing guns,
She'd put up a sturdy fight.

The British ships engaged her,
Firing high to smash her masts,
Bellerophon and *Leander*
Sharing constant cannon blasts.

The sea was now a whirlpool,
Whipped to a creamy foam,
As British ships smashed through French lines,
Their advantage to drive home.

The air was thick with billowing smoke,
And the crash of ships colliding,
As English oak slick-wet with spray,
Down Frenchies' side came sliding.

It was in this heat of battle then,
As the British forged ahead,
That Nelson felt a searing blow
Twixt his eyebrow and his head.

Blinded by blood and sweat and smoke,
Nelson staggered half a pace.
A metal fragment from a shot
Had sliced into his face.

But luck was on brave Nelson's side,
The wound was not severe,
Although at first his desperate thought,
Was the end of his career.

Two sailors helped him to his feet,
And took him down below,
Where Nelson quickly realised,
It was not a serious blow.

He saw the surgeons working there,
Among the maimed and dead.
'Let those men be attended to,
Let them be helped instead.'

Thus Nelson waited for his turn,
While seated on a chest,
But after they had stitched him up,
He still refused to rest.

Meantime the battle raged anew,
As the French now took a battering,
Unprepared as they were, on their landward side,
'Twas from here that their loss was shattering.

Outfought, outflanked, their fleet in flames,
Only two ships escaped slaughter,
By swiftly cutting cables loose,
They sailed to safer water.

While against this might canvas,
This portrait of defeat,
The French, though brave, had to accept,
The destruction of their fleet.

On his flagship Admiral Brueys,
Commander of the French,
Sat wounded on the quarterdeck,
Surrounded by death's stench.

His legs were severed at the knee,
And tourniquets applied,
But after rallying briefly,
This brave French Admiral died.

Throughout the night the bloody fight
Continued without quarter.
Three thousand Frenchmen killed or drowned,
Was the tally of this slaughter.

Utter defeat for Napoleon's fleet,
Was the price that the French had to pay.
His final solution, and the French revolution,
At a stroke now, had been held at bay.

With Nelson now exultant,
His victory assured,
He dispatched a note to England,
In which he praised the Lord.

Almighty God had blessed this fleet,
He was with us all the while,
His holy hands have guided us,
To the victory of the Nile.

'If I was King of England, I would make you the most noble, puissant Duke Nelson, Marquis Nile, Earl Alexandria, Viscount Pyramid, Baron Crocodile and Prince Victory that posterity might have you in all forms.'

Lady Emma Hamilton, in a letter to Nelson,
26 October 1798

12
HONOUR AND DISREPUTE, 1798–1799

Created Baron Nelson,
A nobleman at last,
This aristocratic title,
Helps him shed his humble past.

King Ferdinand of Naples,
Not one to be outdone,
Makes Nelson Duke of Bronte too,
With an estate there in the sun.

Awards are showered upon his head,
In an ostentatious rush,
And Guzzardi paints his portrait,
Sycophancy with a brush.

Nelson poses in full uniform,
Wearing diamonds and a sword,
Looking every inch the hero,
And a haughty English Lord.

But one morning in Palermo,
While visiting the city,
Lord Elgin meets Horatio,
And opines it is a pity –

That this famous English hero,
Has lost his upper teeth,
Has a film across his good eye,
Which is bloodshot underneath.

'He now looks frail and ancient,
Is as slender as a wrath,
But it's in this little fellow,
We still place our nation's faith.'

But Nelson has been captured
By the glitter of the court,
By Emma's adulation,
In this sun-kissed foreign port.

The First Lord of the Admiralty
And Minister of State
Has been well briefed in London,
On Nelson's fragile state.

He's told of Nelson's arrogance
And mad infatuation,
That's likely soon, to undermine
His heroic reputation.

'Send Nelson off to Malta'
Is the Admiralty plan,
'Let him command the fleet there,
This awkward, brilliant man.'

But Nelson has grown obdurate,
And resolute of will,
He cannot sail to Malta,
For he claims he's very ill.

He'll stay in warm Palermo,
Surrounded by his friends,
Nursed back to health by Emma Dear,
Till his fragile body mends.

But Lord Spencer at the Admiralty
Is not to be denied,
He knows that Nelson's true excuse,
Is to stay by Emma's side,

'You must not lie inactive,
In that distant foreign port,
Resign at once and come straight home,'
Is Lord Spencer's stern retort.

Faced with this ultimatum,
Nelson knows he must obey.
He resigns command as ordered,
And prepares to sail away.

But Emma now is pregnant,
And Sir William, showing tact,
And knowing Nelson is the sire,
Seems impervious to the fact.

But as so often in the past,
Coincidence propitious,
Reveals that Emma too will leave,
A prospect quite delicious.

Sir William will accompany her,
As they journey home by sea.
Thus Nelson and both Hamiltons
Make up a cosy three.

But the promise of an ocean trip,
Fills Emma Dear with dread.
She pleads, she squeals and she appeals,
'Go overland instead.'

This change of plan accepted,
By both Nelson and by Emma,
They organise their party now,
To proceed without dilemma.

Their journey is most leisurely,
Quite like a royal train,
With pauses in great capitals,
To alleviate the strain.

In Florence and Vienna,
Their reception is sublime,
For Nelson is a hero,
A legend of his time.

Festivities and fireworks,
Parades and feasts and balls
Are thrown to honour Nelson,
In flag-bedecked great halls.

But mixed with the hosannas,
Adulation and the cheers,
Remarks are made about the pair,
That soon reach Nelson's ears.

Observers note that Emma
Is behaving to a pattern.
She is gross and vile and vulgar,
With the language of a slattern.

But others say that Nelson too
Seems quite devoid of grace,
Both pompous and vainglorious,
With a pinched and waxy face.

He clearly is besotted,
By his bloated lady love,
As she flatters him and coos at him
Like a monstrous turtle dove.

Their journey ends, as jouneys do,
And from Hamburg they are sailing,
The last few leagues to England now,
With Nelson, gaunt and ailing.

Though still a British hero
And a lion of the seas,
The scandal of his love affair
Is the cause of great unease.

His faithful wife awaits him,
'Tis a meeting full of dread,
Fanny feels their love is over,
It's a lonely path she'll tread.

Although he knows in England,
Social battles must be fought,
For he finds a cool reception
In his Sovereign's Royal Court.

But time's a faithful healer,
And men's memories are short,
He'll be hailed, not as adulterer,
But for the battles that he's fought.

13

COPENHAGEN, 1801

A call to arms for Nelson
After months of land-locked life,
Was a clarion note most beautiful,
That replaced domestic strife.

He'd bade farewell to Fanny,
For his heart was pledged to Emma,
The decision had been sorrowful,
But extinguished his dilemma.

Now summoned to the Baltic,
By the Admiral Hyde Parker,
His mission to confront the Danes,
As war prospects grew much darker.

The Scandinavians seemed intent
To thwart the British fleet,
By blocking all attempts by them,
The Frenchmen to defeat.

The Baltic States, including Danes,
Had formed a neutral force,
Designed to hamper British ships
And harry them off course.

The British ultimatum,
Unambiguous and clear,
Was for Danish ships to stand aside,
Or face consequence severe.

Sir Hyde Parker, the Commander,
Felt a blockade might suffice,
But Nelson favoured action,
Were they men or were they mice?

The Danish ships' formation,
Was defensively deployed
In the 'King's Deep' city waters,
Where they were soon to be destroyed.

Aboard the good ship *Elephant*,
Nelson led the first assault,
Pouring broadside after broadside
At the anchored Danes off port.

Amid the smoke and cannon fire
Of this fierce British attack,
Hyde Parker signalled Nelson
To desist, and then draw back.

But Nelson ever obstinate,
Was unable to comply,
He viewed the Admiral's signal
With his famous blind right eye.

He turned to Captain Foley,
Who was standing on his right,
'You know old boy, it sometimes helps
If you don't have perfect sight.'

'I really cannot help it
If the signal is obscure,
So continue with the action
Till surrender we procure.'

Although the Danes fought bravely,
Their losses were severe,
To capitulate before too late
Was now quite crystal clear.

Triumphant now aboard his ship,
The Danish foe destroyed,
He went ashore to meet the Danes,
His diplomacy deployed.

In England news soon reached them,
Of Nelson's mighty feat,
How acting on initiative
He'd subdued the Danish fleet.

And Admiral Hyde Parker,
Though a decent man it's true,
Would evermore his caution
And his timidity rue.

For Nelson would replace him
As Commander of the fleet.
He'd soon be made a Viscount,
His triumph now complete.

14

BULLOCKS, ONIONS AND WINE, 1804

Lord Nelson's concern for his ships and his men
Was confirmed by his notes and dispatches.
No detail was missed, no item too small,
As he ordered supplies in large batches.

His note to the chief agent victualler
For the Mediterranean fleet,
Listed all that he needed, and had to be heeded,
Delivered on time – and complete.

The agent, a fellow named Ford,
When receiving commands from his Lord,
Proceeded with haste, there was no time to waste,
As if urged by a prod from a sword.

The list of supplies was prodigious,
Tons of apples, salt pork and twine,
Sheep by the dozen and carrots,
Plus bullocks and onions and wine.

Fresh fruit was required to fight scurvy,
Spanish oranges, juicy and ripe,
And the wine came in casks of old timber,
But was bought in those days by the 'pipe'.

Rice, sugar and sacks of dried raisins,
And pepper and tallow and rum,
This was all to be paid by the agent,
With real money, a capital sum.

For Nelson, a stickler for detail,
Knew supplies were a key to success,
And that sailors well fed, and properly led,
Would fight better than if they'd had less.

15

MONSIEUR LA TOUCHE TRÉVILLE, 1804

On the afternoon of 14 June 1804, eight French ships came out of Toulon and Nelson, with only five sail of line, formed in order to receive them. But the French returned to port. Nelson assumed this was just a show of strength, a 'gasconade', and did not pursue the French to port. Later, Admiral La Touche Tréville asserted that Nelson had 'run away' and that after 'pursuing the British' saw 'no more of them' the next day – a clear accusation of cowardice which incensed Nelson. He rebutted the charge in a letter to the Admiralty in July.

> A letter can hurt like a bullet,
> And words can cut deep as a blade,
> When honour's at stake, it's a wicked mistake,
> To write lies that put truth in the shade.
>
> No flesh wound or cut is so deadly,
> No musket ball striking to maim,
> Can deliver such pain and such anguish,
> As a blow that destroys a man's name.
>
> On a fine summer's day just off Toulon,
> The French fleet was resting in port,
> Commanded by Admiral Tréville,
> A clever, vainglorious sort.
>
> Aware that the British were waiting,
> Flags aloft 'gainst horizon and sky,
> He'd cock them a snook, from his place on the poop,
> By raising his topsails up high.

But Nelson was not to be ruffled,
As the Frenchmen lay pretty and neat,
With their ships lined up just as sunset
Streaked the heavens with colours discreet.

Nelson hoped that if he could tempt them,
To once leave the safe haven of port,
He'd engage them with skill, then move in for the kill,
'Twixt five ships of the line they'd be caught.

But Tréville himself was not tempted,
To swallow the rich British bait.
He'd bob and he'd weave, and then take his leave,
While Nelson, frustrated, would wait.

Eight sail of the line and six frigates,
Cutting capers just south of the shore,
Nelson's view 'twas just harmless manoeuvres,
A mere 'gasconade', surely, no more?

No shots were exchanged, and no broadsides,
No musket fire, cannon or gun,
Just the billowing sails of the Frenchmen
As they turned portwards, lit by the sun.

But when Admiral Tréville, that saucy old devil,
Prepared his official dispatch,
His message was plain, giving Nelson much pain,
Saying Horatio deserted his patch.

Though Nelson's response was quite icy,
His language was sharp and direct,
'To imply that I'd fly, is a monstrous black lie,
My behaviour was strictly correct.'

Nelson came by the French Admiral's letter,
The one containing the lies,
And he wrote to his brother in England,
Claiming he'd be revenged by and by.

'I keep the letter safe,' he wrote,
'But if perchance we meet,
I'll stuff the letter down his throat,
His black lie he will eat.'

But it, perhaps, was for the best,
The two men never met,
For Tréville died the following year,
With no murmur of regret.

16

MEDICINE AT SEA

Each royal naval surgeon
With his warrant* and degree,
Was as vital as a gunner
When our warships went to sea.

Equipped with awesome instruments
And medicines galore,
They'd heal the sick and wounded,
Who would queue outside their door.

Some ailments sailors suffered from
Were trivial and mild,
Seasickness – not surprisingly,
Known as 'bearing Neptune's child'.

A draught or two of seawater,
Or 'aether' in a glass,
Peruvian bark or purging salts,
Would help the nausea pass.

Camomile and senna leaves,
Mustard seed and nitre,
Sometimes a dose of laudanum,
To calm a half-crazed fighter.

Sarsaparilla, mercury,
Opium and brandy,
This latter was most popular
When no other cure was handy.

* In 1793 there were 550 surgeons in the navy. By 1806, 720. They all held university degrees and had been examined by the Court of Examiners of the Company of Naval Surgeons before receiving a warrant of appointment from the Navy Board.

The surgeon's tools were plentiful,
And kept all shiny bright,
For they were in continuous use,
During every naval fight.

Forceps for the arteries,
The metacarpal saw,
Tourniquets and needles,
'Bone nippers' for the jaw.

Scalpels shaped like cutlasses,
Lancets, probes and scoops,
Trusses, splints and bandages,
Swabs and cranial hoops.

All amputations done at sea,
Were commonplace and quick.
There were no anaesthetics then
To ease pain – or help the sick.

Those surgeons were a feisty crew,
All heroes every one,
As they deployed their bloody skills,
In rain or wind or sun.

Old sailors still salute them,
Remember them with pride,
Recall those distant glory days,
Serving England side-by-side.

17

THE TWO HEROES MEET

In the year of our Lord, eighteen hundred and five,
Was a date to be dearly remembered,
Where Lord Nelson himself and his stouthearted tars,
Saw the French and their fleet quite dismembered.

It was in that same year in September,
Just before the great battle began,
That Nelson encountered in London,
Another extraordinary man.

'Twas autumn and the leaves were all turning
To colours of ochre and red,
And the nation was buzzing with rumour,
Of troubles that still lay ahead.

Would the French ships invade us from Calais?
Would Napoleon dare to strike now?
Would each English village be subject to pillage?
Would the sword be replacing the plough?

The Colonial Office in Whitehall,
Was an edifice noble and grand,
Where the lofty affairs of the Empire,
Were assumed to progress and expand.

It was here in a room unpretentious,
By a window that looked on the street,
That two heroes of England were destined,
For the first and the last time to meet.

For Wellington, not yet a duke,
First impressions were quite painful,
He found the little Admiral,
Both pompous and disdainful.

Vainglorious and a charlatan,
Who boasted all the while,
In a manner starkly opposite
To Wellington's sombre style.

But by the time they'd parted,
And gone their separate ways,
Wellington had decided
That his views he'd re-appraise.

He saw how Nelson's knowledge
Had embraced affairs of state,
How his single-minded focus
Would protect olde England's fate.

And so they never met again,
After that autumn day,
Perhaps in paradise they talk
While celestial trumpets play.

18

TRAFALGAR, 21 OCTOBER 1805

Upon this famous, fateful day,
Spread out across the ocean,
The ships appear like flocks of birds,
White-winged in gentle motion.

Ahead the French and Spanish fleet,
All men and weapons ready,
Observe the British ships approach,
And the order's given – 'steady.'

Admiral Villeneuve, their leader,
A sailor brave and true,
Sees Nelson's battle plan quite plain,
It's to cut his line in two.

He issues orders to his staff,
He knows that time is short,
'Wear together – go about,
Lest by Nelson we'll be caught!'

The French ships and the Spanish
Now make a turnabout,
Pursued by Nelson at three knots,
Too slow to make a rout.

But even at this gentle pace,
With wind behind each sail,
The British tactics are most bold,
Men pray they will not fail.

Some time beyond eleven hours,
With high clouds scudding by,
Nelson sends a signal out
That becomes a rallying cry.

'England expects that every man –'
Is the stirring opening phrase,
Designed to stiffen sinews
And low spirits swiftly raise.

The enemy fleet is turning fast
To form a concave bow,
Towards this centre Nelson moves,
But his progress is still slow.

At noon the fight commences,
White ensigns hoisted high,
The mighty ships move closer,
As fresh winds begin to sigh.

And then like devil's breath exhaled
Across the glimmering sea,
A pall of acrid gunsmoke drifts
As far as the eye can see.

As canvas snaps and timbers creak,
Above the ocean's roar,
Cannonballs like meteorites,
From the cannon's mouth now pour.

Upon the heaving, groaning decks,
Lies a scattering of sand,
It's there to soak up sailors' blood,
As by their guns they stand.

The mighty vessels toss and weave,
From forests they've been built.
From oak and other noble trees,
They roll and pitch and tilt.

The splintered spars and fraying ropes,
Collapse upon the decks,
But still the sweating matelots
Perform their gun drill checks.

Prepare to load, protect your ears,
The ramrods driven home,
And then like bucking iron mules
The guns fire o'er the foam.

Sails sodden now and slashed to shreds,
As frigates swift and sleek,
Manoeuvre in the briny spume
Advantage there to seek.

Royal Sovereign led by Collingwood,
Is in a most ferocious fight,
She's crippled *Santa Ana,* but
There's more French on her right.

Five ships at least start blasting
At *Sovereign's* decks and siding,
Hot shells from hell explode pell-mell,
Some in mid-air colliding.

Belleisle engages *Fougueux,*
But her mizzen mast is split,
She's raked by Frenchies' cannon fire
And takes a crippling hit.

Her bowsprit and her figurehead
Are shot away and shattered,
Her hull is smashed and splintered
And her decks with blood are spattered.

But midst the cries of dying men,
And the cannon's deafening crack,
A seaman's pike is raised up high,
Topped by a Union Jack.

Now *Victory* herself is caught
In a murderous hail of fire
As she lies perpendicular,
She can't shoot – she can't retire.

Her rigging has been damaged,
She's exposed to broadside shot,
Alas, among the casualties
Is Nelson's secretary, Scott.

From high up in the rigging,
Comes a deadly blast of hail,
And a fusillade of chain-shot
That rips clean through the sail.

French gunners mark their targets
And reload to fire again,
When above the roar of shot and shell
Comes a human scream of pain.

A midshipman's been wounded,
A splinter's pierced his chest,
He staggers on the slick-wet deck,
Blood spouting through his vest.

The ship has tilted starboard,
And loose tackle starts to slide,
As the dying young midshipman
Is hurled over the side.

For a moment he's suspended
In the seething foam-tipped waves,
Like a cork that's been up-ended,
Above countless sailors' graves.

Then the mighty deep engulfs him,
And he vanishes from view,
Soon to kneel before his maker
On eternal heaven's pew.

As Nelson turns to Hardy,
He gives a rueful smile,
'This is warm work,' he says,
'And can last but just a while.'

Although his flagship's under fire,
French gunnery is slack,
Made worse by the ocean's rising swell
And the *Victory*'s fighting back.

The French and Spanish officers,
Now watch each move aghast,
As *Victory* shifts position,
Returns fire and sails straight past.

She's heading for a cluster
Of French and Spanish ships,
But Hardy warns his Admiral,
'We'll strike upon their hips!'

'We'll run aboard – we'll hit them',
Is Hardy's earnest shout,
But Nelson doesn't hesitate,
He will not turnabout.

No dodging or manoeuvring now
As from her larboard side,
The *Victory* fires a cannonade,
The Frenchmen cannot hide.

Revenge is sweet and justified,
As *Bucentare* takes a hit,
So close, its tattered ensign
Almost touches Nelson's ship.

Bucentare's out of action now,
Her score of guns dismounted,
The loss of men she's suffered too,
Four hundred dead, when counted.

And *Victory* is not herself unscathed,
With broken spars and rigging,
But she's firing fast on all her guns,
Her mood is not forgiving.

Redoubtable, a fine French ship,
Is spoiling for a fight,
She pulls alongside *Victory*,
So close, they're locked in tight.

So close indeed, like Siamese,
Who share a common hip,
That men can see their rivals' eye,
And their perspiration drip.

For fully fifteen minutes now,
There's lethal, murderous firing,
And midst the noisome smoke and flame,
Brave men collapse, expiring.

Sharp tongues of flame and plumes of smoke,
Leap 'twixt the rolling ships,
As matelots on either side
Strive hard to get to grips.

Then midst the noise and turmoil,
On *Victory*'s heaving deck,
Nelson appears in uniform,
Decorations round his neck.

A target unmistakable,
Our Admiral of the Fleet,
Is this the awful moment then,
When his destiny he'll meet?

He's struck, he falls like a smitten oak,
The ball has sunk in deep,
A mortal blow, the final one,
As angels, unseen, weep.

He's carried at once to the orlop deck,
Below *Victory*'s waterline,
And as surgeon Beatty examines him,
He knows there's little time.

He feels the surge and gush of blood,
In the cavity of his chest,
His spine is shattered fatally,
Three hours to live at best.

The strength is draining from him now,
And with Hardy at his side,
He speaks of Lady Hamilton
With tenderness and pride.

He knows he's served his country well,
For his God and for his King,
Says Hardy, as he clasps his hand,
'Good tidings, Sir, I bring'.

'The battle's won,' says Hardy,
And he kisses Nelson's cheeks.
'Thank God I've done my duty then',
Are the last words Nelson speaks.

19

THE KING'S NAVY

Colossus, Achilles and proudly named *Mars,*
Gliding swift on the ocean 'neath the clouds and the stars,
The *Queen* and the *Dreadnought* with their topsails serene,
All these ships manned by matelots, doughty and keen.

Neptune and *Canopus, Spencer* and *Prince,*
All resolved to a man not to give Frenchie an inch,
Zealous and *Donegal, Swiftsure, Orion,*
Each ship made of oak with the heart of a lion.

Africa, Conqueror, Ajax, Defiance,
All perfect examples of nautical science,
Spartiate, Tigre, Agamemnon exquisite,
And HMS *Victory* – which today we still visit.

Bellerophon, Minotaur, Tonnant, Defence,
All sleek in the ocean with firepower immense,
Glorious *Britannia* and *Thunderer* too,
With wind in their sails and stern duty to do.

Leviathon, Temeraire shared in their fame
As they scudded o'er waves to join the great game,
Royal Sovereign, Revenge, Prince of Wales and the rest,
As England expects nothing less than the best.

Polyphemus and *Belleisle* make up the great fleet,
As just off Cadiz French ships they soon meet,
With flagships and cutters and frigates galore,
To mark up once more a great victory score.

Britannia exultant, the enemy routed,
As from village and hillside the word 'Victory' is shouted,
The French fleet destroyed, invasion plans spoiled,
Napoleon's ambition comprehensively foiled.

Let hosannas be sung, though they'll be mixed with tears,
For most of the dead are of young tender years,
Look up to the heavens, past clouds, smoke and spray,
Give thanks for our Navy this glorious day.

Though canvas may split and timbers will rot,
The deeds done this morning will not be forgot.
To that host of dead heroes, let our prayers never cease,
With Horatio Nelson – may they all rest in peace.

20

LAST VOYAGE

To be buried at sea with old shipmates,
And his body consigned to the deep,
Seemed an inappropriate ending
For the man for whom England would weep.

So his body was lifted by sailors,
And placed gently inside a large cask,
Which was filled to the brim with fine brandy,
Willing hands then completed the task.

In this large wooden barrel of liquor,
Lord Nelson was carried back home,
Transferred in a coffin to Greenwich,
To the Great Painted Hall – all alone.

Here the public in thousands came to mourn him,
The Princess of Wales at their head,
Paying tribute to England's great sailor,
Who to victory our nation had led.

His memory remains quite unblemished,
Though the passage of years slips on past,
And seafarers all will fondly recall
His name, as they raise up their glass.

To honour him still and remember,
Remark how he always walked tall,
Lord Horatio Nelson, the sailor,
England's Admiral admired most of all.

21

THE FRENCHMAN WHO SHOT NELSON

He sits in a tavern in Calais,
Taking sips of his vin ordinaire,
But his grey eyes are shifty as ferrets,
And he nervously tugs at his hair.

The wax on his pigtail is limp now,
And his old face is weathered and tanned.
From his tattered right sleeve, a hook we perceive
That replaces what once was his hand.

His jacket is faded and threadbare,
His breeches are greasy and worn,
And the lines on his face make it so hard to place,
What his age is or where he was born.

Though the tavern is crowded and noisy,
And the smoke from the pipes fills the room,
He remains in his place with no smile on his face,
Drinking wine in the gathering gloom.

No fellows attempt to approach him,
No comrades, no barmaid, no whore,
As he swallows his drink with a flourish,
And stares sightlessly up at the door.

But at length when his bottle is empty,
He lurches out into the night.
The cobbles are shiny with rainfall
And the wind has a sharp winter bite.

He walks slowly across to the dockside,
Where the water is choppy with foam,
And he sits on a bollard beside it,
Like a man taking ease when he's home.

But his mind is elsewhere in a turmoil,
Full of images bloody and stark,
And a coachman who passes by slowly,
Hears the old man call out in the dark.

'A hit,' he cries up to the heavens,
But his voice is cracked and weak,
'A hit I say, mon Dieu, mon Dieu!
With my Emperor let me speak!'

The coachman pulls his reins in,
And his horses snort and stamp.
Who is this loon? this old poltroon
Who gabbles by the lamp?

The coach wheels begin turning,
As he gives his whip a flick,
He'll leave the old man to himself,
He's crazy and he's sick.

Alone again and muttering,
His body tensed with pain,
The old man screams, as hideous dreams
Rush in and fill his brain.

And now the images grow bright,
They dance before his eyes,
He sees heaving, foamy oceans,
Hears dying sailors' cries.

'Mon Dieu, I beg,' he calls again,
'Pray let me die for France,
I've done my duty honestly,
With ne'er a backward glance.'

'Yea, on the ship *Redoubtable*,
Midst that final bloody fight,
I did what I did for my country,
I did what I thought was right.'

'I'm high up in the rigging,
Above the smoke and noise,
I can see the struggle down below,
The men look small, like toys.'

'And then a figure on the deck,
Quite different from the rest,
Appears in shiny uniform,
Gold medals on his chest.'

'White stockings and blue breeches,
And gleaming buckled shoes,
Mon Dieu, it's him, it's Nelson,
Here's a chance I cannot lose.'

'I raise my musket slowly,
And peer along its length,
The wind howls through the rigging,
Holy Mother, give me strength.'

'I squeeze the trigger slowly,
There's a blast and puff of smoke,
The burning powder scorches me,
And I begin to choke.'

'I nearly lose my footing,
And clutch the rigging tight,
But as the smoke is blown away,
The scene below is bright.'

'For Nelson lies spreadeagled,
Upon the heaving deck,
My musket ball has struck him hard,
High up, close to his neck.'

'I see the gouts of blood appear,
And stain his jacket red,
"My backbone is shot through," he cries,
He's wounded, but not dead.'

'And then the hounds of hell appear,
And swarm aboard our ship,
The heavy waves pound at our helm,
And we begin to tip.'

'A hundred British matelots
With cutlasses and guns,
Are hacking at our seamen,
Dear France's bravest sons.'

'The scene is one of carnage,
As sabres clang like bells,
And musket fire like thunderclaps
Is mixed with human yells.'

'I feel my fingers slipping,
I can't retain my grip,
And then I lose my footing
And crash down upon the ship.'

'I think my back is broken,
I can scarcely draw a breath,
While around me sweating bodies
Are fighting to the death.'

'I struggle to stand up again,
But the decks are slick with blood,
I fall again, like a ragged doll,
With a monumental thud.'

'Above me as I flounder,
I perceive an awesome sight,
An Englishman is straddling me,
His eyes are fierce and bright.'

'He wields a heavy cutlass,
It twirls above his head.
I know that in a moment's time,
I surely will be dead.'

'But he too loses balance,
And slithers on the deck,
I heave myself towards him
And seize him by the neck.'

'But he is far too quick for me,
And his body gives a twist,
Then he slices through my outstretched arm,
At the joint of hand and wrist.'

'But now the dream is fading,
The visions disappear,
I can't recall what happens next,
Or when, what month or year.'

'But this I know for certain,
No man believes my tale.
They say I'm just a sailor
Who's too sick and old to sail.'

'But I'm that cursèd Frenchman
Who shot Lord Nelson dead.
It's true, I swear, not fantasy
That swirls inside my head.'

'But I am very tired now,
And people say I'm mad,
No pension or reward for me,
No medals to be had.'

'But I'm that cursèd Frenchman,
Who shot Lord Nelson dead,
Will someone please believe me
And honour me instead.'

22

LAMENT FOR AN OLD SALT

There's a matelot from Portsmouth,
Name of Jim,
Though he's sailed the seven seas,
He still can't swim.

He tells tales that make your eyes grow wide with wonder,
And he claims he's even heard a mermaid sing,
He's seen places quite exotic, and met women most erotic,
In the service of old George, his Sovereign King.

He's got muscles on his back like bloomin' Atlas,
And his hands are strong thru' pulling hard on ropes,
He's a rough and ready tar, having travelled near and far,
And it's on him that old England pins her hopes.

He's a gunner and he's seen a lotta fighting,
He's heard cannon fire a thousand times or more,
He's seen bloodshed, he's seen death, felt the tropic wind's
hot breath,
And when he quits the navy, he'll be poor.

He admits that he has done his share of plunder,
And he keeps his coins and trinkets in a tin,
But on a foreign shore, he won't spend it on a whore,
Though confessing that a little goes on gin.

With his belly full of rum, he will stand beside his gun,
With the look-outs yelling 'enemy in sight'.
Battle still gives him a thrill, an' he knows his cannon drill
Will prove better than the Frenchman's in a fight.

He was out there in the Battle of Trafalgar,
Midst the gun smoke and confusion and the noise,
He's seen men cut in half, staunched mates' bleeding with
his scarf,
And watched sailors killed, no more than beardless boys.

But he's old now and he's looking very fragile,
As he sits out on the porch, it makes you sad,
For his moods these days are sunk in reminiscence,
I don't mind though – for you've guessed it, he's my Dad.

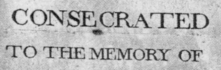

CONSECRATED

TO THE MEMORY OF

LORD VISCOUNT NELSON

BY THE ZEALOUS ATTACHMENT

OF ALL THOSE WHO FOUGHT AT

TRAFALGAR

TO PERPETUATE HIS TRIUMPH

AND THEIR REGRET

MDCCCV

23

HYMN TO A DEAD HERO

When Nelson died, his soul ascended
To a life in heaven, that's never ended,
Around him choirs of angel's sing,
And goblets of ambrosia bring.

His duty done to God and King,
His spirit craves just one last thing.
May all his deeds be long remembered
By scribes of history not dismembered.

Though centuries pass and memories falter,
Let Nelson's story never alter.
On each October, autumn day,
Let men remember, pause and pray.

And out upon King Neptune's seas,
'Neath billowing cloud and ocean breeze,
Let sailors of all ranks and ages,
Be keen to study history's pages.

Be certain sure they know the story
Of the man who brought Old England glory.
And never let those memories dim
Of good Horatio, God bless him.